THE BEHAVIORAL RESPONSE OF
WEALTH ACCUMULATION TO ESTATE TAXATION:
TIME SERIES EVIDENCE

by
David Joulfaian
US Department of the Treasury

OTA Paper 96   November 2005

OTA Papers is an occasional series of reports on the research, models, and datasets developed to inform and improve Treasury's tax policy analysis. The papers are works in progress and subject to revision. Views and opinions expressed are those of the authors and do not necessarily represent official Treasury positions or policy. OTA Papers are distributed in order to document OTA analytic methods and data and invite discussion and suggestions for revision and improvement. Comments are welcome and should be directed to the authors.

Office of Tax Analysis
US Department of the Treasury
1500 Pennsylvania Avenue, NW
Washington, DC 20220

The paper benefited from comments by Gerald Auten and Robert Carroll for helpful comments. The valuable research assistance of Margaret Rolley is gratefully acknowledged. Comments are welcome to david.joulfaian@do.treas.gov.

The Behavioral Response of Wealth Accumulation to Estate Taxation:
Time Series Evidence

Abstract

This paper explores the behavioral response of taxable bequests to estate taxation. To gauge its effects, the estate tax is converted to an equivalent income tax. This highlights the importance of expected rates of return, and also makes it possible to compare effective tax rates on saving over time. Using data on federal revenues from the estate tax over the past 50 years, and employing the equivalent income tax rate measure, the findings suggest that estate taxes have a dampening effect on the reported size of taxable estates. Estate taxation seems to depress taxable bequests by some 14 percent.

Keywords: Saving, Bequests, Taxes
JEL: D19, H31

I. Introduction

Capital taxes create disincentives for saving. Income taxes, such as those that apply to capital gains, interest, and dividends, create disincentives to save by reducing rates of return. Similarly, estate and inheritance taxes may create similar disincentives for the bequest motivated saver (Fiekowsky, 1966; Poterba, 1997). With its repeal on the agenda, as provided for in The Economic Growth and Tax Relief Reconciliation Act of 2001 (EGTRRA), understanding the effects of the estate tax on wealth accumulation is important.

While the disincentives created by capital taxes are clear, a priori, the theoretical effect of these taxes on donors is ambiguous and depends on the offsetting substitution and income effects. More specifically, it depends on the preferences of the potential saver. In the presence of altruistic bequests, for instance, Caballe (1995) and Laitner (2000) simulate the estate tax to have a depressing effect on the capital stock. Similarly, Gale and Perozek (2001) argue that the effects on saving depend critically on the underlying transfer motives. Ultimately, however, the effect of estate taxation is an empirical question. One is tempted to rely on the findings in the literature on the effects of income taxes.[1] But because bequest taxes apply to the stock of terminal wealth, they may not be directly comparable to the income tax that applies to the return to saving or income flows during the life cycle.

The scarcity of data on the size and distribution of wealth spanning different tax regimes, particularly for the wealthiest segment of society, has limited the thorough study of the effects of estate taxation. Holtz-Eakin and Marples (2001), for instance, employ the Health and Retirement Survey panel data (HRS), where the wealthy are under represented, to explore the effect of estate taxes on wealth accumulation. They find estate and inheritance taxes to have a depressing effect on wealth accumulation.

---

[1] For the taxable income response see Feldstein (1995), Auten and Carroll (1999), Carroll (1998), Gruber and Saez (2002), and Kopczuk (forthcoming). For the effects on savings, see Bernheim (1999).

Others resort to administrative data. In the most recent study on the effects of the estate tax on wealth accumulation in the US, Kopczuk and Slemrod (2001), hereafter KS, employ estate tax data for the pre-war period, and augment them with limited data for the post war years.[2]

In an earlier study, Chapman, Hariharan, and Southwick (1996), hereafter CHS, explore how estate taxes affect post war federal government estate and gift tax revenues. In modeling the effects of estate taxes on wealth accumulation, CHS make creative use of annual time series data on federal estate and gift tax revenues. Lacking individual level data, they regress these annual collections on an imputed contemporaneous measure of the estate tax rate. They report tax rates to have a negative effect on this source of revenues to the government.[3] The major limitation of this paper is that the dependent variable is the combined sum of estate and gift taxes, two variables that do not always move in tandem and are governed by different tax regimes. Indeed the spike that CHS report in fiscal year 1977 has little to do with estate taxes; it is explained by the acceleration of gifts in 1976 with gift taxes paid in 1977 (Joulfaian, 2004a).[4]

KS pursue two strategies in examining the effects of the estate tax on wealth. First, they expand on CHS and employ time series analysis using aggregate wealth reported on estate tax returns for the years 1916 through 1945, and select post war years. Using three measures of the tax rate, the maximum, and those imputed for 40 and 100 times per capita wealth, KS report a negative correlation between the share of top wealth-holders and the estate tax rates. This contemporaneous relationship holds controlling for a number of other influences. A similar sentiment is expressed in Kopczuk and Saez (2004)

---

[2] Generally reliable cross sectional estate tax data are available for deaths in 1982 and most of later years. Reliable data is also generally available for the years 1962, 1969, 1972, and 1976. For prior years, data is available for the period 1917 through 1945.

[3] While the authors report findings on the contemporaneous effects of taxes, their estimates actually reflect a forward looking process as the lead tax rate is employed. Tax collections usually lag the liability year. Much of the collections in fiscal year 1990, for instance, reflect wealth and tax liability in calendar year 1989. Thus their specification generally tests, for example, whether the tax rate in 1990 affected wealth reported in 1989.

[4] The maximum gift tax rate increased from 57.75 in 1976 to 70 percent in 1977.

as they contrast the share of household wealth held by the wealthiest estates with contemporaneous estate tax rates.

In the second strategy, KS resort to pooled cross-sectional analyses that make use of individual estate tax returns. Unlike their time series analysis, the effects of the contemporaneous estate tax rate on the size of reported wealth is weak. However, they find much stronger effects when the tax rate is measured using laws that prevailed at age 45 or ten years before death. The estimates from their preferred specification imply that a tax rate of 50 percent reduces reported wealth by about 10.5 percent.

The cutting edge work of KS in exploring pooled data is quite formidable, particularly when compared to their time series analysis as well as that of CHS. Indeed, it is not clear how to interpret the findings from the time series analysis on the effects of contemporaneous tax rates or the econometric problems of time series estimation in general (Auerbach, 2001). How does the tax regime in effect at death explain wealth accumulated during life? After all, if the focus is on wealth accumulation, the behavioral response and estate planning must have preceded the date of death. Thus, KS's analysis of the pooled data and the effects of lagged tax regimes should be viewed as a significant contribution to the literature.

Comparisons of trends in wealth accumulation over time is quite challenging, in particular as gift taxes did not apply prior to mid 1932.[5] The easiest way to avoid estate and inheritance taxes is through tax-free lifetime gifts, unless this is checked by the imposition of gift taxes. It is noteworthy that during the congressional deliberations in 1932 to increase the maximum estate tax rate from 20 to 45 percent, and the introduction of a gift tax regime, one individual is reported to have made about $100 million in gifts; another to have made gifts of about $50 million (Roosevelt, 1938: 312). Considering that the entire yield of the estate tax in 1932 was $400 million, the tax-free inter-vivos transfers of $150 million by these two individuals alone, not to mention likely gifts by

---

[5] The federal government introduced a gift tax in 1924 which was repealed in 1926.

4

scores of others, demonstrate the likely sizeable leakages from the estate tax in the early years of its enactment. These leakages make intertemporal comparisons a challenging undertaking, and may produce biased behavioral estimates when periods with and without gift tax regimes are included in the same sample.

In addition to the gift tax regime, and as noted in Auerbach (2001), relying on pre-war data to aid in gauging the effects of the estate tax can be problematic. Also, and as argued in Clotfelter (1985, pp. 240), given the frequent pre-war changes in tax laws, it is not clear which tax regime is driving behavior. Changes in the definition of residency as well as in the tax base only add to this challenge.[6]

In this paper I address the effects of estate taxation by examining data on federal government revenues from the estate tax for the fiscal years 1949 through 2001, which correspond to terminal wealth in the years 1948 through 2000. I also develop measures of estate tax equivalent income tax rates to gauge the effects of taxation over time. The equivalent income tax rate is the rate that applies to the annual return on an asset that leaves the size of an heir's inheritance unaffected. For a given estate tax rate, the equivalent income tax rate is low during periods of high rates of return expectations, and vice versa. The reported evidence is suggestive of a stronger estate tax effect when using the equivalent income tax measure, and much weaker when the estate tax rate itself is used.

This paper is organized as follows. Section II provides an overview of trends in estate tax collections by the federal government, and the evolving tax regimes. Section III discusses how estate taxes can be analyzed as an equivalent income tax. It also describes the data sources and explains the construction of variables. Section IV presents empirical evidence on the effects of the estate tax. The findings are sensitive to specification and

---

[6] The introduction of the US Treasury Liberty Bonds and, subsequently, Flower Bonds which may be viewed as a prepayment, albeit at a discount, of estate taxes (bonds as a form of life insurance), further complicates intertemporal comparisons. Similar complications are introduced by the treatment of pensions and annuities.

the measure of the estate tax rate employed. A concluding comment is provided in section V.

II. Background

Federal estate tax revenues grew steadily in the post-war period. As shown in Figure 1 and Table 1, estate tax revenues grew from near a billion in 1948 to $25 billion in 2000. Adjusted for inflation, however, the implied growth rate is less impressive.[7] Real tax revenues grew through the early 1970s, and precipitately declined in the following years. It was not until the late 1990s that the real levels of the early 1970s were attained. When stated relative to GDP (Figure 2), or relative to household net worth as in Figure 3, revenues grew over the years but never regained the peak collections of the early 1970s. On average, estate taxes represent one quarter of one percent of GDP, and less than one tenth of one percent of the Flow of Funds household wealth.

Studying the revenue streams depicted in Figures 1-3 is not directly helpful in gauging the effects of taxes on accumulated wealth. In particular, economic growth and the evolving structure of the estate tax make it rather difficult to gauge such effects. While inflation adjusted estate tax revenues grew by 376 percent in this period, for instance, the real gross domestic product grew by some 500 percent and US Household net worth and the S&P index grew even faster.

As for the estate tax structure, major changes in tax regimes took place in 1977, 1982 through 1987, and to a lesser extent in 1998 and beyond.[8] The size of exempted estate from estate taxation remained at $60,000 through 1976. The exemption was replaced by a unified tax credit which effectively doubled the exemption in value in 1977, and greatly expanded it between 1982 and 1987 to $600,000. In real terms, however, the exemption

---

[7] Again, these actually refer to fiscal years 1949 and 2001. Tax collections usually lag liabilities, reflecting filing requirements. Estate tax collection data is obtained from the IRS Annual Report of the Commissioner (various years) as well as the IRS Data Book (various years).

[8] These include the Tax Reform Act of 1976 (TRA76), the Economic Recovery and Tax Act of 1981 (ERTA81), and the Taxpayer Relief Act of 1997 (TRA97).

fell in value in the early years, expanded from 1977 through 1987, and then fell again as shown in Figure 4. Other things equal, this had the effect of expanding the tax base in the earlier as well as later years.

In this period under study, the maximum estate tax rate was reduced from 77 to 70 percent in 1977. It was further reduced to 55 percent, but leaving much of the schedule for lower brackets intact. The introduction of the unified credit, however, effectively reduced the marginal tax rates in the lowest brackets to zero.

Another significant tax reduction took place in 1982, when spousal transfers became exempt from tax. In 1981 and prior years, the deduction for spousal bequests was limited to 50 percent of the estate (as first introduced by the Revenue Act of 1948). But because spousal transfers may potentially enlarge the estate of the surviving spouse, they do not necessarily escape taxation.[9] This, at least in part, may explain the growth in revenues in the late 1980s and 1990s as more and more of the estates of surviving spouses became subject to the estate tax. Table 2, which reports information on the life expectancy of surviving spouses, illustrates the potential for recapture of the expanded marital deduction. And Figure 5 depicts the effective rate for the unlimited marital deduction pre and post ERTA81.[10]

III. Modeling the effects of estate taxation

Much of the wealth held by the very wealthy becomes subject to the estate tax at death. In many ways, the tax can be viewed as an excise tax on large bequests. This tax, which applies once to accumulated savings, is not directly comparable to the income tax which may apply annually to the return on savings. More specifically, the burden of the estate

---

[9] Throughout this period state Elder Laws, which dictate pre-set amounts or shares of estates to be set aside for the surviving spouse, were also changing further confounding the measurement of the effects of estate taxation.

[10] This represents an attempt to control for statutory changes in the allowed marital deduction. Of course there is no guarantee that the surviving spouse won't spend down her wealth. To make post 1981 data comparable to prior years, the marital deduction for this period is set equal to $0.5 + 0.5*(1-m)$ of the estate, where m is the cumulative probability of death of the surviving spouse.

tax, unlike that of the income tax, may vary with the rate of return and the age of the bequest motivated saver.

To facilitate comparisons, this "excise" tax on bequests can be restated as an equivalent income tax that applies to annual accruals of the income on savings. Assuming the bequest motive is the sole purpose for saving, a wealth holder is indifferent between an estate tax that applies to bequests at death and a lifetime annual equivalent income tax on the return to accumulated wealth that leaves the size of transfers to the heirs unaltered.

Algebraically, with a marginal estate tax rate e, estate tax equivalent income tax rate τ, expected rate of return r, and life expectancy or holding period n, we should expect the following to hold for wealth saved today:

$$(1+r)^n(1-e) = [1+r(1-\tau)]^n \qquad (1)$$

That is, an individual may save \$1 today and leave $(1+r)^n(1-e)$ to his heirs in period n. Under an equivalent income tax regime, the heirs receive $[1+r(1-\tau)]^n$. The latter term, i.e., $r(1-\tau)$ is commonly used in modeling the effects of income taxes on saving. From this identity, the estate tax equivalent income tax rate becomes:

$$\tau = \frac{(1+r)-(1+r)(1-e)^{1/n}}{r} \qquad (2)$$

From equation (2) it follows that, for a given estate tax rate, the equivalent income tax rate declines with life expectancy and the expected rate of return. Alternatively stated, older individuals face a higher equivalent income tax rate. But this rate is lower when higher rates of return are expected.[11]

---

[11] The challenge here is to derive economy wide tax rate to capture differences in life expectancies. Joulfaian (2004b) applies mortality rates to estate tax data to arrive at such a measure. In many ways this is similar to that of Poterba (1997) who applied mortality rates to the living population.

Figure 6 illustrates the influence of age and rates of return on the measured equivalent income tax rate. Consider a male individual expecting to face an estate tax rate of 55 percent. For an individual age 21, with a rate of return of 10 percent on assets and life expectancy of 54.6 years, the equivalent income tax rate on annual earnings is 16 percent. This declines to 7 percent when a rate of return of 25 percent is expected. The respective tax rates become 68 and 31 percent, respectively, in the case of a 71 year old male with a life expectancy of 12.5 years.

In order to derive equivalent income tax rates some measure of the rate of return expected over the remaining life expectancy is needed. For simplicity, in any given year, this measure is defined as the maximum of the 10-year moving average rate of return to equity, measured as the growth rate of the S&P index, and that of after-tax bond yield. The latter is proxied by the municipal bond yield.[12] Figure 7 plots this expected rate of return.

Identifying the tax regime in effect for estate planning purposes is critical. I start with a 10-year lag, but also consider a number of other lags as well. The taxable estate weighted age for decedents in 1998 was about 81.7 years. Life expectancy, again weighted by the size of taxable estates, but evaluated at ten years before death is 15 years.[13] Given that the wealthy experience lower mortality rates than those of the general population (Poterba, 2001),[14] as well as the five year differential above, the life expectancy is more likely to be closer to 20 years. Thus, the equivalent income tax rate is derived using n=20 in equation (2), but n=15 is also considered.[15]

---

[12] Much of the return on equity can be avoided by the step up in basis at death. Replacing municipal bonds with taxable corporate bonds has little effect on the findings.

[13] This is computed using the general population life expectancy. See http://www.cdc.gov/nchs/data/nvsr/nvsr52/nvsr52_14.pdf.

[14] For mortality rates of annuitants, which are much lower than those of the general population, see http://library.soa.org:8080/xtbml/tableList.zip.

[15] The empirical findings are little affected when n=15 years is employed. Ideally life expectancy should vary by the age of the wealth holder, and using a representative measure of life expectancy may lead to aggregation bias.

9

To generate the income tax rates, I first employ the maximum estate tax rate. One drawback of this measure is that it may overstate the expected tax rate faced by the less wealthy. As an alternative, I also employ a predicted estate tax rate measure computed using mean taxable estate values. The latter is derived using a taxable estate of $2.2 million reported by the estates of decedents in 1998. The primary limitation of the latter approach is that it overlooks the reductions in the maximum tax rates that took place over time. And, second, it is difficult to properly identify the representative size of wealth as it is likely to be endogenous to the tax regime in place. Figures 8 and 9 plot the estate tax rates in effect over the period 1948 through 2000, along with the derived measures of the equivalent income tax rates using the rates of return in Figure 7.

IV. Empirical Findings

To gauge the effects of estate taxation, I employ data on federal government estate tax collections for the fiscal years 1949 through 2001. These years correspond to transfers or tax liability in calendar years of 1948 through 2000. First, the stream of revenues is normalized by the estate tax rate, net of the state death tax credit rate, to generate proxies for the taxable estates. The latter is then divided by the Flow of Funds household net worth, represented in the dashed line in Figure 3. Next, I regress this ratio, multiplied by 100, on the estate tax equivalent income tax rate, τ, as defined in (2).

For the regressors, I begin with a measure based on the maximum estate tax rate, and employ a number of control variables. The latter include the real size of the exempted estate. Expansions in the exemption amount should reduce the size of the dependent variable. I also control for the amount of spousal bequests accorded a marital deduction, measured as a fraction of the estate. The greater the fraction of the estate allowed as a marital deduction the smaller is our dependent variable. Other variables include the S&P index to control for stock market appreciation. This index also controls for the effects of corporate and personal capital gains taxes in as far as they affect the return to holding corporate equity. Table 3 provides descriptive statistics.

Beginning with column one of Table 4, the estimated coefficient on the tax rate is negative with a value of -0.025 (se=0.004). Evaluated at the sample mean value of the share of wealth, the taxable estate elasticity with respect to the tax rate is -0.18.[16] This suggests, with the usual caveats, that in the absence of the estate tax, taxable estates may increase by 18 percent.

Moving to the control variables, the size of the estate exemption, as expected, has a dampening affect on the reported taxable estates and the ensuing estate tax revenue. The estimated coefficient is -0.024 (se=0.006). Similarly, and as expected, the marital deduction has a dampening effect on the taxable estate. The estimated coefficient is -0.04 (se=0.02).

Adding a trend variable, or actually year, has little effect on the above estimates, except for the marital deduction where the coefficient is no longer statistically significant (column 2). Little change is also observed in these estimates when the S&P index is considered (column 3). The estimated coefficient on the index is positive, and, not surprisingly, suggests that estate tax wealth rises when the S&P index appreciates. The estimated coefficient on the tax rate is -0.0192 (0.0085), and implies an elasticity with respect of the tax rate of -0.14.

Alternative lags were considered for the specification in column 3. Only the nine-year lag was statistically significant, with almost identical estimates. Of course, ideally all the lagged tax rates should be included in the right hand side as wealth is accumulated over the life cycle. Unfortunately, the correlation between these rates prevents estimation with such a specification.

In column 4 the equivalent income tax rate is replaced with the 10 year lagged estate tax rate. Unlike the previous estimates, the estimated coefficient is now imprecisely measured, with a value of 0.027 (se=0.041). Even though the income tax rate equivalent

---

[16] The elasticity is computed by multiplying the estimated coefficient on the tax rate by the inverse of the wealth share. The mean wealth share, multiplied by 100, is 0.1392 as in table 3.

11

measure is derived using the same measure of the estate tax rate, the estimated effects diverge, highlighting the importance of the rates of return as predicted in equation (2).

One possible limitation of the estimates in Table 4 is that the maximum tax rate may not be the margin at which some plan their estates. As such, the tax rates may be measured with error for these individuals. As an alternative, the predicted measure of tax rates is employed. As a reminder, this measure is based on an average taxable estate of $2.2 million in 1998, and is adjusted for inflation to generate measures of marginal tax rates for the entire sample period.

These estimated coefficients, now reported in Table 5, are significantly different from those reported earlier. They all retain the same sign, but increase in significance and size. Beginning with column 1 of Table 5, the estimated coefficient on the tax rate is -0.076 (se=0.021), implying an elasticity of taxable estates with respect to tax rates of -0.33. The estimated elasticity changes little, and becomes -0.27, when year and the S&P index are included. These estimates also change little when nine and eight year lags are considered, but become insignificant when lags under eight years are considered.

Given that US household wealth itself might be endogenous to taxes, the estimated elasticities reported in Tables 4 and 5 may be biased. [17] Estate tax decedents may very well be representative of the wealthiest segment of the living population. Thus, as an alternative to the above estimates, columns 3 and 4 in Tables 4 and 5 are re-estimated with the dependent variable defined as the log of real taxable estates. The results are reported in Table 6.

In column 1 of Table 6, the estimated coefficient on the equivalent income tax rate is -0.14, and almost statistically significant at the 5 percent level. In this constant elasticity specification, the coefficient implies an elasticity of taxable bequests with respect to the tax rate of -0.14, identical to that in column 3 of Table 4. In column 2, the tax rate

---

[17] Even those not sufficiently wealthy to be subject to taxation, may be affected by the estate tax. Interestingly, a recent CBS News/ New York Times poll found that 71 percent of Americans favored eliminating the tax. http://www.cbsnews.com/stories/2001/03/14/politics/main278884.shtml.

variable is based on the predicted estate tax rate. The estimated effect of the tax rate is virtually unchanged, and again implies an elasticity ofm-0.14. This, however, is in absolute terms smaller than the -0.27 reported in column 3 of Table 5. Columns 3 and 4 replace the equivalent income tax rate with the estate tax rate directly. Again, and as in column 4 of Tables 4 and 5, the estimated effects of the estate tax rate are not precisely measured.

V. Conclusion

This paper explored the effects of estate taxation on bequests using time series data for the period 1948 through 2000. It derives an income tax equivalent measure of the estate tax rate which allows for the effects of estate taxes to vary with the expected rate of return.

Depending on the specification employed, the estimated elasticity of the taxable estate with respect to the equivalent income tax rate is between -0.14 and -0.27. In other words, and with the usual caveats, the taxable estate is 14 to 27 percent smaller because of the estate tax.[18] However, there is greater support for the finding of an elasticity of -0.14. As with much of the work on the taxable income elasticity, it is not clear whether this measures the effects on saving and wealth accumulation, or reflects tax avoidance (Slemrod, 2001). As one example, minority discounts claimed on estate tax returns filed in 2001 reduce taxable estates by about three percent. In the absence of the estate tax, there will be no longer a need to engage in estate planning and employ strategies designed to reduce the reported value of assets. Nevertheless, and as pointed out by Feldstein (1999), both types of response reflect a welfare cost of estate taxation.

---

[18] Note that some of the reduction in taxable estates may be recaptured under the income tax. Inflated executor commissions paid to a relative, for instance, are taxed under the income tax as compensation. Similarly, undervaluation of estates may lead to greater capital gains realizations by the heirs.

References

Auerbach, Alan (2001). "Comments: The Impact of the Estate Tax on Wealth Accumulation and Avoidance Behavior," in Rethinking Estate and Gift Taxation, William G. Gale, James R. Hines Jr., and Joel Slemrod, editors, Washington, DC: The Brookings Institution Press.

Auten, Gerald and Robert Carroll (1999). "The Effect of Income Taxes on Household Behavior," Review of Economics and Statistics, November, 81 (4), 681-693.

Bernheim, B. Douglas, (1999) "Taxation and saving," NBER Working Paper 7061.

Bernheim, Douglas B. (1987). "Does the Estate tax Raise Revenues?" in Tax Policy and the Economy 1, National Bureau of Economic Research, Cambridge, Massachusetts.

Carroll, Robert (1998). "Do Taxpayers Really Respond to Changes in Tax Rates? Evidence from the 1993 Act," Office of Tax Analysis Working Paper 78, U.S. Department of Treasury.

Chapman, Kenneth, Govind Hariharan, and Lawrence Southwick Jr. (1996). "Estate Taxes and Asset Accumulation," Family Business Review 9 (Fall), 253-68.

Clotfelter, Charles T. (1985). Federal Tax Policy and Charitable Giving, University of Chicago Press, Chicago.

Feldstein, Martin S. (1995). "The Effect of Marginal Tax Rates on Taxable Income: A Panel Study of the 1986 Tax Reform Act," Journal of Political Economy, June, 103 (3), 551-572.

Feldstein, Martin S. (1999). "Tax Avoidance and the Deadweight Loss of the Income Tax," Review of Economics and Statistics, November, 4 (81), 674–680.

Fiekowsky, Seymour (1966). "The Effects on Saving of the United States Estate and Gift Tax," in Federal Estate and Gift Taxes, edited by Carl Shoup, Washington, DC: Brookings Institution.

Gale, William G. and Maria G. Perozeh (2001). "Do estate Taxes Reduce Saving?" in Rethinking Estate and Gift Taxation, edited by William G. Gale, James R. Hines, and Joel Slemrod, Washington, DC: Brookings Institution.

Gruber, Jon and Emmanuel Saez (2002). "The Elasticity of Taxable Income: Evidence and Implications," Journal of Public Economics, April, 84 (1), 1-32.

Holtz-Eakin, Douglas and Donald Marples (2001). "Distortion Costs of Taxing Wealth Accumulation: Income Versus Estate Taxes," NBER Working Paper No. 8261, April.

14

Internal Revenue Service, Data Book, various years.

Internal Revenue Service, Annual Report of the Commissioner of the Internal Revenue, various years.

Joulfaian, David (2005). "Choosing between Gifts and Bequests: How Taxes Affect the Timing of Wealth Transfers," forthcoming in Journal of Public Economics, NBER working paper 11025.

Joulfaian, David (2004a). "Gift Taxes and Lifetime Transfers: Time Series Evidence," Journal of Public Economics, 88:9-10, August, 2004, 1917-1929.

Joulfaian, David (2004b). "How Estate Taxes Can be Stated as Income Tax Equivalent Taxes," Office of Tax Analysis, US Department of the Treasury, June, mimeo.

Joulfaian, David (1998). "The Federal Estate and Gift tax: Description, Profile of Taxpayers, and Economic Consequences," OTA Paper no. 80, U.S. Department of the Treasury, December.

Kopczuk, Wojciech (forthcoming). "Tax Bases, Tax Rates and the Elasticity of Reported Income," Journal of Public Economics.

Kopczuk, Wojciech and Emmanuel Saez (2004). "Top Wealth Shares in the United States, 1916-2000: Evidence from Estate Tax Returns," National Tax Journal, lvii:2, Part 2, 445-487.

Kopczuk, Wojciech, and Joel Slemrod (2001). "The Impact of the Estate Tax on Wealth Accumulation and Avoidance Behavior," in Rethinking Estate and Gift Taxation, William G. Gale, James R. Hines Jr., and Joel Slemrod, editors, Washington, DC: The Brookings Institution Press.

Poterba, James (2001). "Estate and Gift Taxes and Incentives for Inter Vivos Giving in the US," Journal of Public Economics, 79(1), January, pp. 237-64

Poterba, James (1997). The Estate Tax and After-Tax Investment Returns, NBER working paper 6337, Cambridge, Massachusetts.

Roosevelt, Franklin D. (1938). The Public Papers and Addresses, v.5, Random House, New York, 312-14

Slemrod, Joel (2001). "A General Model of the Behavioral Response to Taxation," International Tax and Public Finance, 8(2), 119-28.

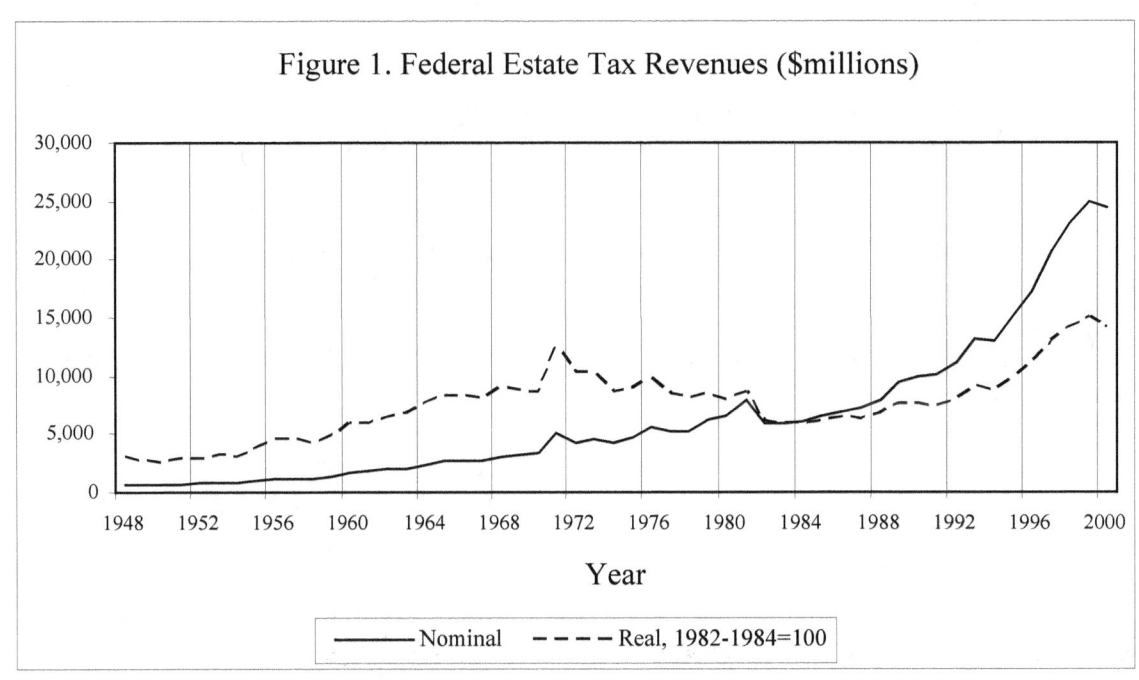

Figure 1. Federal Estate Tax Revenues ($millions)

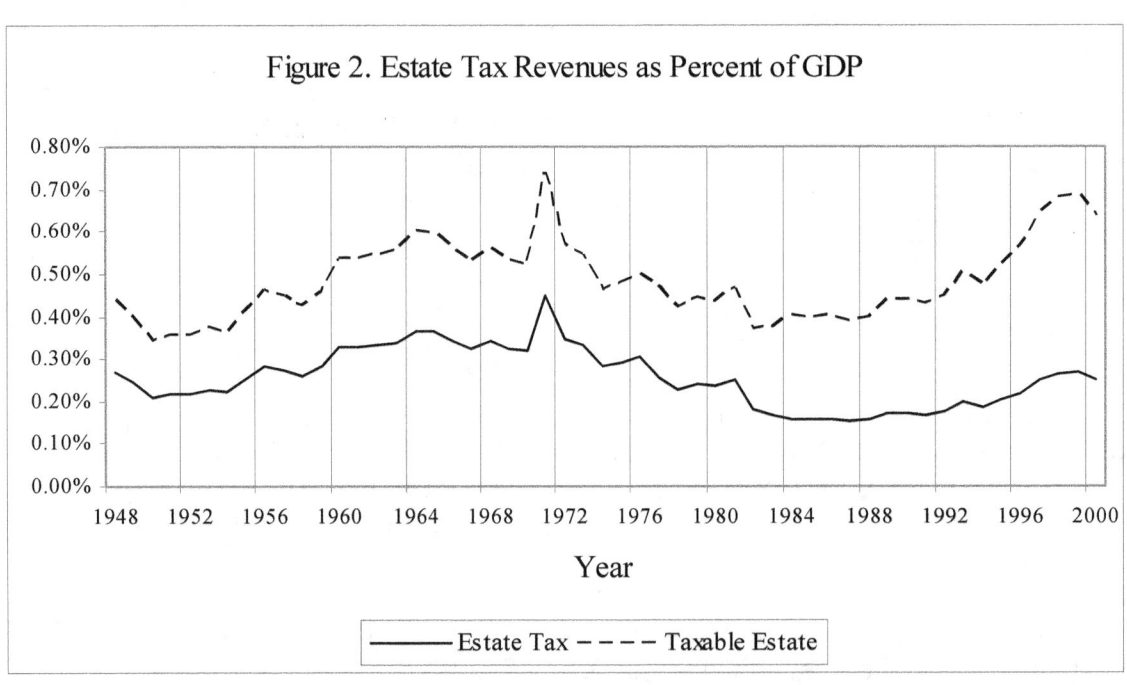

Figure 2. Estate Tax Revenues as Percent of GDP

16

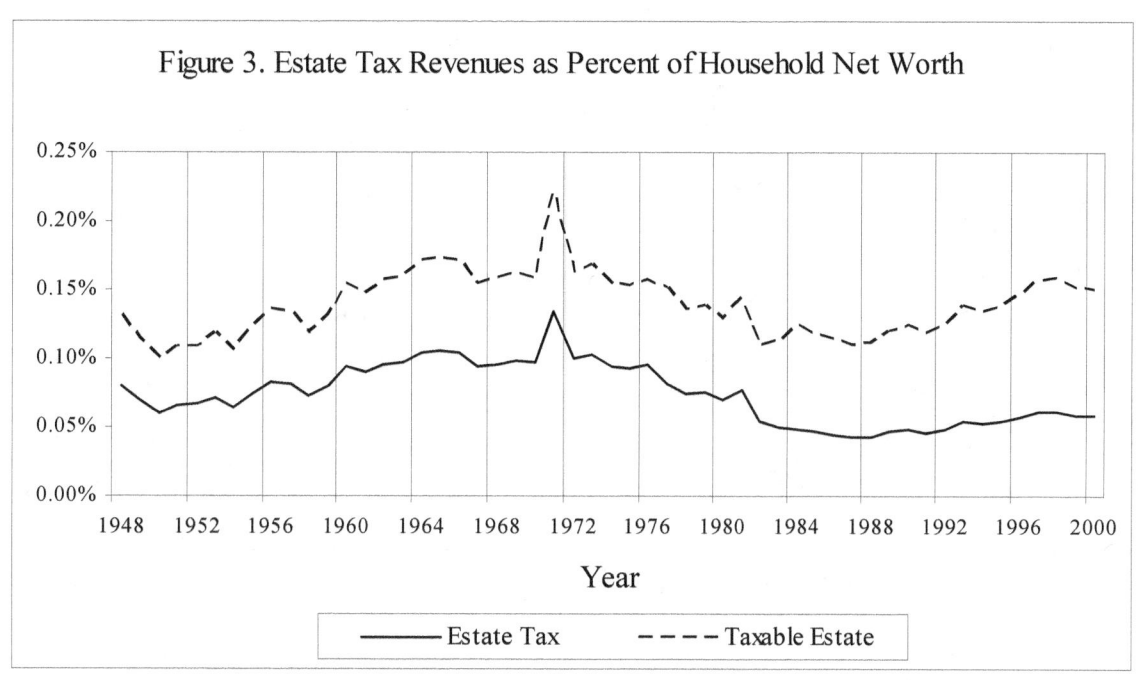

Figure 3. Estate Tax Revenues as Percent of Household Net Worth

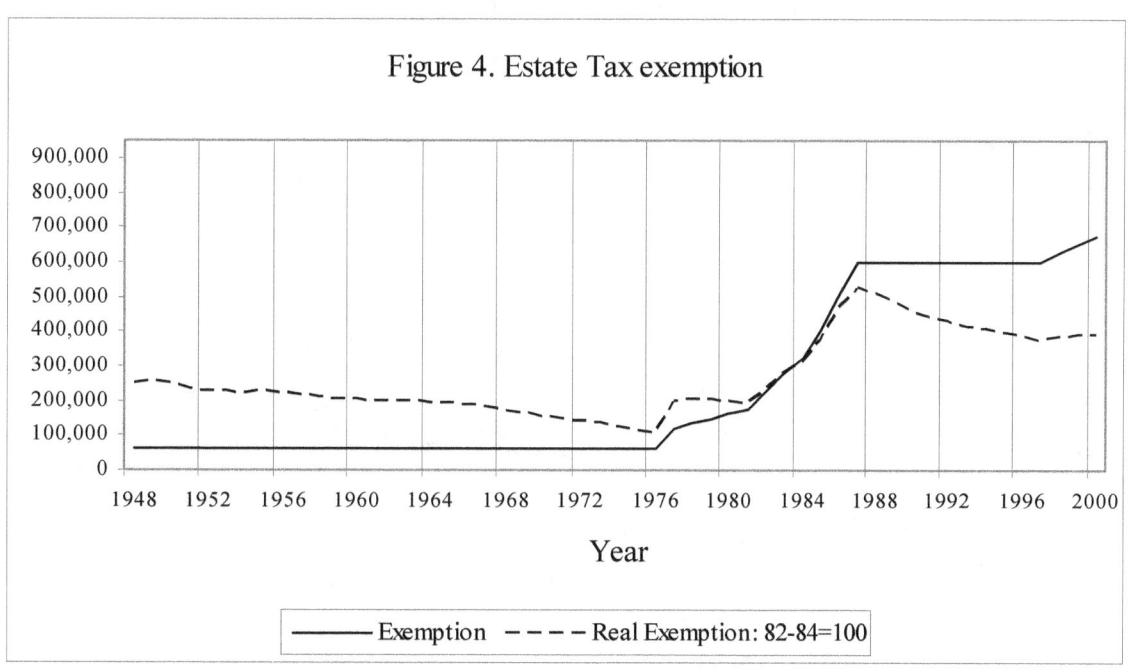

Figure 4. Estate Tax exemption

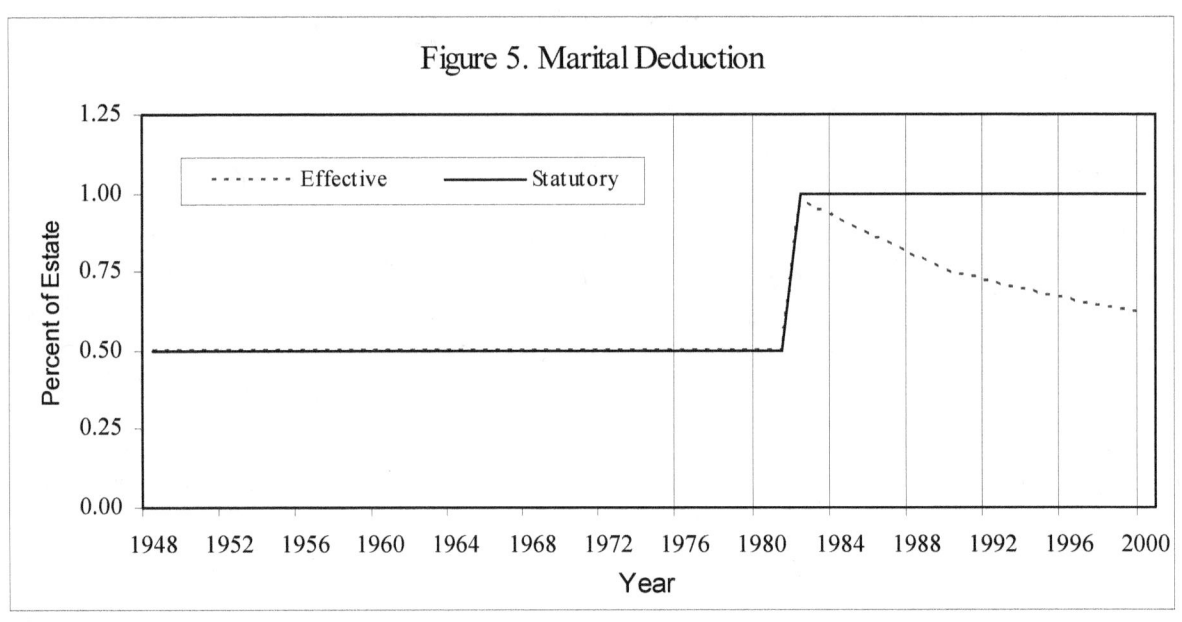

Figure 5. Marital Deduction

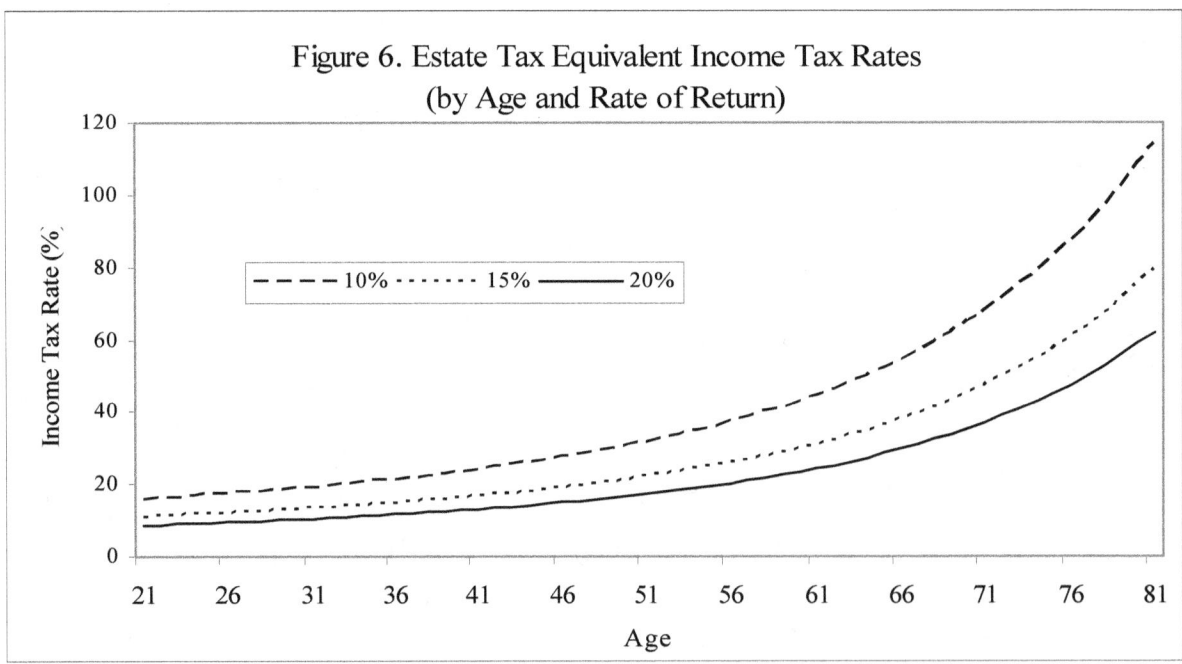

Figure 6. Estate Tax Equivalent Income Tax Rates
(by Age and Rate of Return)

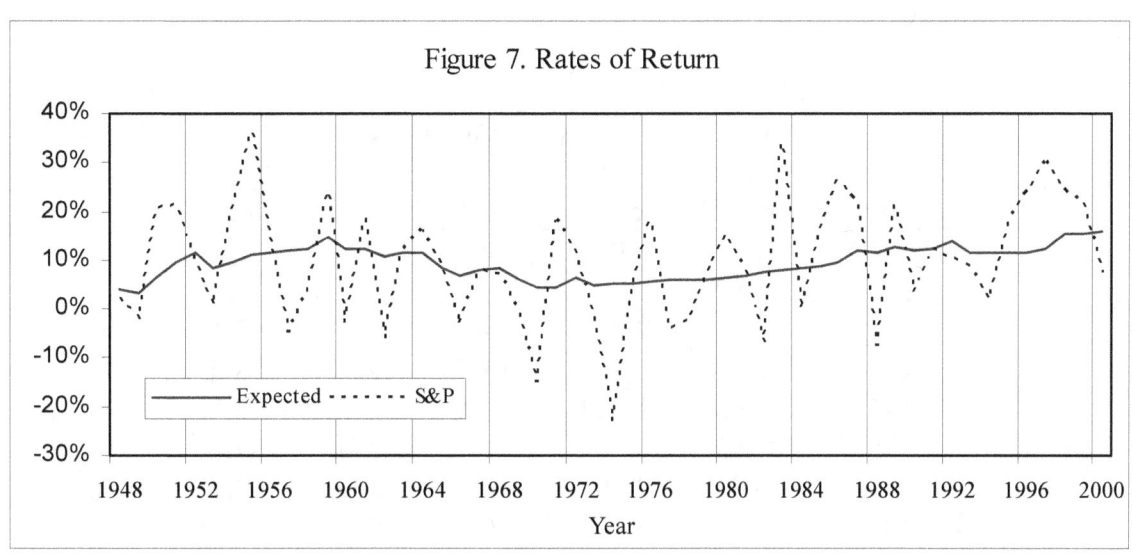

Figure 7. Rates of Return

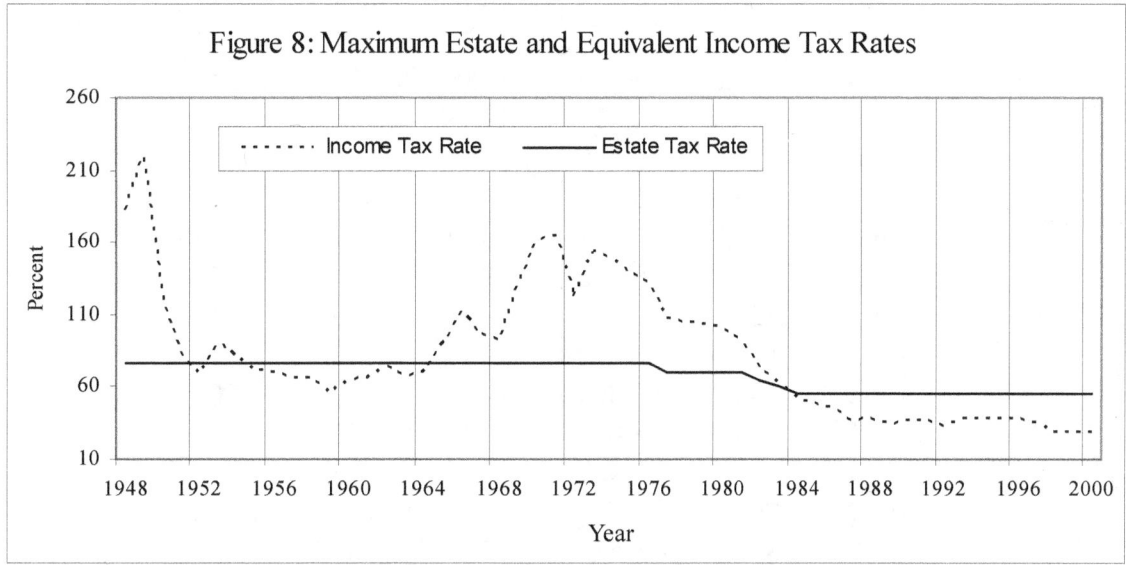

Figure 8: Maximum Estate and Equivalent Income Tax Rates

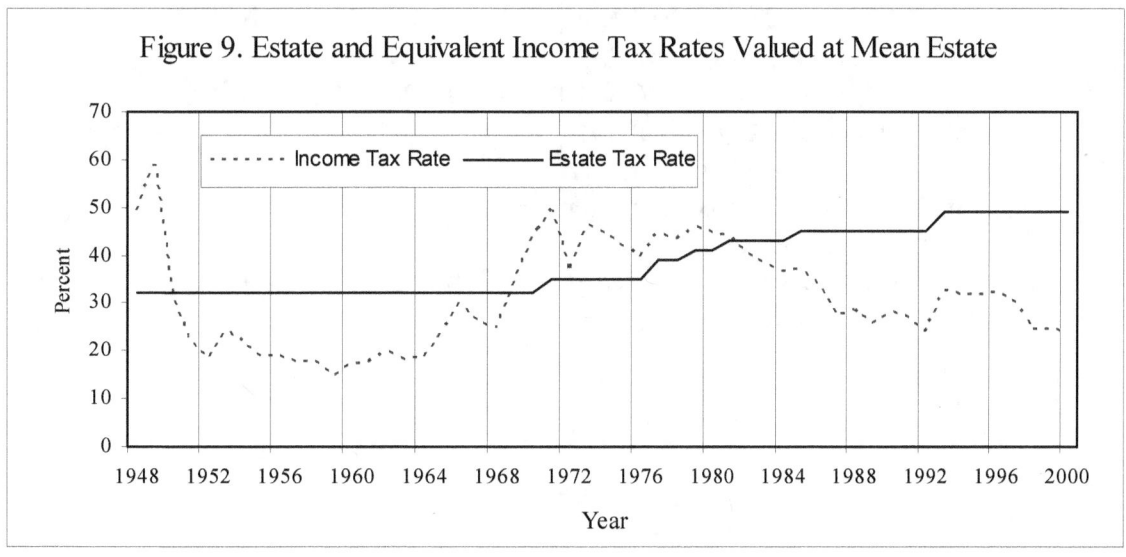

Figure 9. Estate and Equivalent Income Tax Rates Valued at Mean Estate

Table 1

Estate Tax Revenues ($millions)

Year*	Nominal	Real**	Year*	Nominal	Real**
1948	719.3	2,984	1975	4,784.3	8,893
1949	649.2	2,728	1976	5,551.1	9,756
1950	616.8	2,559	1977	5,145.6	8,491
1951	735.4	2,829	1978	5,236.1	8,031
1952	774.3	2,922	1979	6,172.9	8,503
1953	862.2	3,229	1980	6,571.3	7,975
1954	836.2	3,109	1981	7,883.0	8,672
1955	1,047.6	3,909	1982	5,904.3	6,118
1956	1,240.1	4,559	1983	5,858.3	5,882
1957	1,259.1	4,481	1984	6,145.7	5,915
1958	1,215.8	4,207	1985	6,577.5	6,113
1959	1,418.9	4,876	1986	6,990.0	6,378
1960	1,725.1	5,828	1987	7,167.6	6,309
1961	1,777.0	5,943	1988	7,915.5	6,691
1962	1,951.2	6,461	1989	9,371.8	7,558
1963	2,088.7	6,826	1990	9,903.1	7,577
1964	2,424.8	7,822	1991	10,099.3	7,415
1965	2,619.0	8,314	1992	11,140.5	7,940
1966	2,692.2	8,309	1993	13,136.3	9,091
1967	2,679.3	8,022	1994	12,965.0	8,748
1968	3,097.6	8,901	1995	14,975.0	9,826
1969	3,205.2	8,734	1996	17,136.0	10,922
1970	3,303.4	8,514	1997	20,787.0	12,951
1971	5,072.6	12,525	1998	23,136.0	14,194
1972	4,280.1	10,239	1999	24,926.0	14,962
1973	4,594.2	10,347	2000	24,441.0	14,193
1974	4,235.6	8,591			

* Lagged fiscal years, proxy for calendar year liabilities.
** Using CPI 82-84=100.
Source: Internal Revenue Service, Annual Report of the Commissioner, various years, and Data Book, various years.

Table 2

Life Expectancy of Surviving Spouses

Years*	Relative Frequency	Cumulative Relative Frequency
<1	0.042	0.042
1	0.063	0.105
2	0.064	0.169
3	0.054	0.223
4	0.066	0.289
5	0.059	0.348
6	0.054	0.402
7	0.058	0.459
8	0.047	0.506
9	0.033	0.539
10	0.034	0.573
11	0.031	0.604
12	0.026	0.630
13	0.027	0.656
14	0.025	0.681
15	0.025	0.706
16	0.022	0.729
17	0.020	0.748
18	0.021	0.770
19	0.016	0.785
20	0.016	0.802
21	0.013	0.815
22	0.017	0.832
23	0.019	0.851
24	0.012	0.863
25	0.014	0.877
26	0.015	0.892
27	0.010	0.903
28	0.013	0.916
29	0.007	0.923
30	0.013	0.936
30+	0.064	1.000

* Distance between deaths of first and second spouse.
  Obtained from estate tax returns of decedents in 1995.

Table 3

Descriptive Statistics

Variable	Mean	Std Dev	Min	Max
Year	1974	15.44345	1948	2000
Estate Tax ($mil)	6,359	6,270	617	24,926
Taxable Estates ($mil)	14,622	16,751	1,011	63,913
Percent of GDP (%)	0.4836	0.0928	0.3439	0.7379
Percent of Household Net Worth (%)	0.1392	0.0232	0.0994	0.2209
Maximum Estate Tax Rate (%)	68.74	10.08	55.00	77.00
Net Estate Tax Rate (%)	52.74	10.08	39.00	61.00
Equivalent Income Tax Rate (%)	81.66	44.74	28.48	219.84
Exemption Amount	240,645	240,870	60,000	675,000
Real Exemption	267,146	114,421	105,448	528,169
Marital Deduction (%)	59.3	14.2	50.0	97.9
S&P Index	228	316	15	1,427
S&P Moving Average Growth Rate	0.09	0.04	0.00	0.16
Expected Rate of Return (r)	0.09	0.03	0.03	0.16
Real GDP ($Bil)	4,711	2,316	1,634	9,817
Household Net Worth ($Bil)	10,580	11,553	894	42,332
CPI	73.21	50.00	23.80	172.20
Tax Variables Computed at Mean Taxable Estate				
Taxable Estate ($mil)	17,269	14,784	2,084	60,795
Percent of GDP (%)	0.7973	0.2897	0.3917	1.4519
Percent of Household Net Worth (%)	0.2329	0.0897	0.1110	0.4346
Estate Tax Rate (%)	38.30	6.73	32.00	49.00
Net Estate Tax Rate (%)	33.37	4.84	28.80	41.80
Equivalent Income Tax Rate (%)	31.15	10.61	14.82	59.26

Table 4

The Determinants of the Ratio of Taxable Estates to Household Wealth, 1948-2000
(Using maximum estate tax rate; coefficients followed by standard errors in parentheses)

Variable	(1)	(2)	(3)	(4)
Intercept	0.4556*	1.0417*	1.0449*	0.3635
	(0.0682)	(0.4766)	(0.4720)	(0.6762)
In Estate Tax Rate $_{t-10}$	--	--	--	0.0272
	--	--	--	(0.0409)
In Equivalent Income Tax Rate $_{t-10}$	-0.0248*	-0.0282*	-0.0192*	--
	(0.0044)	(0.0052)	(0.0085)	--
In (Real Exemption)	-0.0235*	-0.0195*	-0.0261*	-0.0332*
	(0.0062)	(0.0069)	(0.0085)	(0.0084)
Marital Deduction %	-0.0398*	-0.0304	-0.0212	-0.0280
	(0.0192)	(0.0205)	(0.0215)	(0.0242)
In Real S&P	--	--	0.0129	0.0340*
	--	--	(0.0098)	(0.0082)
Year	--	-0.0003	-0.0003	0.0000
	--	(0.0003)	(0.0003)	(0.0003)
Elasticity	-0.18	-0.20	-0.14	0.20
Adjusted R^2	0.7136	0.7175	0.7230	0.6883
Observations (regression)	42	42	42	42

* Significant at the 5 percent level, ** at the 10 percent level.

Table 5

Determinants of the Ratio of Taxable Estates to Household Wealth, 1948-2000
(Using a predicted estate tax rate; coefficients and standard errors in parentheses)

Variable	(1)	(2)	(3)	(4)
Intercept	1.5901*	7.7784*	9.0923*	8.8519*
	(0.2355)	(0.7981)	(0.9089)	(1.8742)
ln Estate Tax Rate $_{t-10}$	--	--	--	-0.1083
	--	--	--	(0.1132)
ln Equivalent Income Tax Rate $_{t-10}$	-0.0765*	-0.0873*	-0.0624*	--
	(0.0206)	(0.0129)	(0.0156)	--
ln (Real Exemption)	-0.1090*	-0.0422*	-0.0721*	-0.1035*
	(0.0195)	(0.0148)	(0.0182)	(0.0215)
Marital Deduction %	-0.1617*	-0.1136*	-0.0573	-0.0412
	(0.0595)	(0.0376)	(0.0416)	(0.0493)
ln Real S&P	--	--	(0.0369*	0.0825*
	--	--	(0.0145)	(0.0163)
Year	--	-0.0036*	-0.0042*	-0.0040*
	--	(0.0005)	(0.0005)	(0.0008)
Elasticity	-0.33	-0.37	-0.27	-0.47
Adjusted R^2	0.8475	0.9463	0.9481	0.9274
Observations (regression)	42	42	42	42

* Significant at the 5 percent level, ** at the 10 percent level.

Table 6

Determinants of the *ln* Real Taxable Estates, 1948-2000
(Coefficients and standard errors in parentheses)

Variable	(1)	(2)	(3)	(4)
Intercept	10.2904*	10.0271*	9.8077*	10.3568*
	(1.4998)	(1.4973)	(1.5330)	(1.8043)
ln Estate Tax Rate $_{t-10}$	--	--	-0.2136	0.3816
	--	--	0.5426	0.5601
ln Equivalent Income Tax Rate $_{t-10}$	-0.1377**	-0.1372**	--	--
	(0.0776)	(0.0823)	--	--
ln (Real Exemption)	-0.2746*	-0.2714*	-0.2499*	-0.2528*
	(0.1191)	(0.1190)	(0.1232)	(0.1232)
Marital Deduction %	-0.5512*	-0.5638*	-0.4776*	-0.4733*
	(0.2041)	(0.2041)	(0.2075)	(0.2079)
ln Real S&P	0.4279*	0.4434*	0.4411*	0.4338*
	(0.1037)	(0.1042)	(0.1107)	(0.1119)
Elasticity	-0.14	-0.14	-0.21	0.38
Adjusted R^2	0.9066	0.9064	0.8992	0.8994
DW	2.1028	2.055	2.0084	2.0088

Columns (1) and (2) replicate column (3) in Tables 4 and 5, while (3) and (4) replicate column (4) in Tables 4 and 5. Estimates corrected for autocorrelation with AR(1).

* Significant at the 5 percent level, ** at the 10 percent level.

Recent OTA Working Papers
http://www.treas.gov/offices/tax-policy/library/otapapers/index.shtml

Number	Authors	Title	Date
95	David Joulfaian	Basic Facts on Charitable Giving	06/05
94	Curtis P. Carlson	The Effect of the 2001 Recession and Recent Tax Changes on the Corporate Alternative Minimum Tax	06/05
93	Curtis P. Carlson	The Corporate Alternative Minimum Tax, Aggregate Historical Trends	06/05
92	David Joulfaian	Estate Taxes and Charitable Bequests: Evidence from Two Tax Regimes	03/05
91	Warren B. Hrung	Information, the Introduction of Roths, and IRA Participation	12/04
90	Janet G. McCubbin	Optimal Tax Enforcement: A Review of the Literature and Practical Implications	12/04
89	Scott Jaquette Matthew Knittel Karl Russo	Recent Trends in Stock Options	03/03
88	Peter Brady Julie-Anne Cronin Scott Houser	Regional Differences in the Utilization of the Mortgage Interest Deduction	08/01
87	Robert Rebelein Jerry Tempalski	Who Pays the Individual AMT?	06/00
86	David Joulfaian	Choosing Between Gifts and Bequests: How Taxes Affect the Timing of Wealth Transfers	05/00
85	Julie-Anne Cronin	U.S. Treasury Distributional Methodology	09/99
84	Laura Power Mark Rider	The Effect of Tax-Based Savings Incentives on the Self-Employed	07/99
83	Joann Weiner	Using the Experience in the U.S. States to Evaluate Issues in Implementing Formula Apportionment at the International Level	04/99
82 Rev.	Nicholas Bull Janet Holtzblatt James R. Nunns Robert Rebelein	Defining and Measuring Marriage Penalties and Bonuses	11/99
81 Rev.	Jerry Tempalski	Revenue Effects of Major Tax Bills	07/03
81	Jerry Tempalski	Revenue Effects of Major Tax Bills	12/98
80	David Joulfaian	The Federal Estate and Gift Tax: Description, Profile of Taxpayers, and Economic Consequences	12/98
79	Robert Carroll	Do Taxpayers Really Respond to Changes in Tax Rates? Evidence from the 1993 Tax Act	11/98